A SONG, THE WORLD TO COME

A SONG, THE WORLD TO COME

MIRANDA LELLO

RECENT
WORK
PRESS

A Song, the World to Come
Recent Work Press
Canberra, Australia

Copyright © Miranda Lello 2017

National Library of Australia
Cataloguing-in-Publication entry.

Lello, Miranda
A Song, the World to Come/ Miranda Lello
ISBN:9780995353817 (paperback)

All rights reserved. This book is copyright. Except for private study, research, criticism or reviews as permitted under the Copyright Act, no part of this book may be reproduced, stored in a retrieval system, or transmitted in any form by any means without prior written permission. Enquiries should be addressed to the publisher.

Cover design: Recent Work Press
Set in Bembo 11pt

recentworkpress.com

*For my mum, Beverley,
who loved my poems from
the earliest days*

Contents

1.

That train made from shells

The taste of salt	1
To Mr Charles Bukowski, after 'Swingers'	2
These fragments almost make a poem	4
There is a law of the universe that says no poet dies alone	7
Sometimes it feels like you don't want me anymore	8
These days 1	9
Canberra I: An insomniac welcomes dusk, remembering harder times	10
These days 2	11
There are three things I have to tell you	13

2.

April makes fools of us all

The inside of her	19
Babushka	20
Elegy	21
Startup program WMN-12000	22
some days in autumn my poems don't tell stories	23
Canberra III: all tonight's parties	25
Copan, the ruins	26
The Opposing Shore (after Julien Gracq)	27
Your rock at the end of the world	29
The world on Sir J Herschel's Projection by John Bartholomew	30

3.

The smell of salt

Drinks and chats with old friends	35
The first frost of winter we did not sleep well	36
Atlantis	39
The Lady Vanishing	40
Travelling is nothing like a poem	41
Ghosts and ashes	42
The late night thoughts of a small-minded woman	43
Second person	45
Like a fish on a wire	48

4.

Seekers of the emergency exit

Mexico D.F.	51
The Idiot (Savannah nights)	53
sort of a map of me	54
In the carpark of tomorrow we can all find a parking space	55
Glory be to you who sung *(with Gerard Manley Hopkins)*	*57*
The journey out	58
she walks the long way home	59
A Song, The World to Come	61
Afterword	64

1.
That train made from shells

The taste of salt

There are only seven stories in this world. That
train made from shells you keep to
sing to you—you think like

the ocean whispers time to the
breaking cliffs and the blurring beaches—
sings the same seven stories they play on the TV

In the evening, longing presses
against chambers of ghosts in your chest, who sing
hush, hush, like the sea

There are only seven stories in this world, but
the ocean with each wave touches the land
again for the first time, again

And the taste of salt on skin no wave no ghost can sing

To Mr Charles Bukowski, after 'Swingers'

Women who sleep with too many men are
worn out by all that fucking, all that
rubbing of body against body
tarnishes the softer soul:
makes calluses that appear
on tired eyeballs or painted lips.
Damply parting thighs promise
a moment of hot pleasure
but loose cunts can't make you a god.

Tell me, how can I
count to too many? If I said
I remember every one and that
each time (sometimes with tears some
times with cries and some
simply with a breath and a
shudder) I gave generously and with
some kind of love—
then would it still be
less than that? I concede that
when the trickle down the
inside of my thighs
ceases to feel like tears,
then I will say:
I am like those
men who broke me
their eyes screwed shut,
ungently forcing
an already-open lock. Those men
who sleep with too many women:
men who are dull faced—have
lost the beautiful eyes that see how
each neck arches differently
in tremors of pleasure;

each spine curves in
different lines of submission, of love.

You said women who
sleep with too many men have no
treasures to give: good fortune
for us all there are so many spaces
between Madonna and
Whore, filled with lovers
who have not yet realised
the bed is a battleground
which measures only losses:
all the lovers who never learnt to count.

These fragments almost make a poem

    I. City

In Paris in early summer I scraped the stones
for traces of feet long gone. At the place
called Bastille there is a roundabout and, elsewhere,
the Vendôme column bears no mark of hands
that tore it down; the streets no shadow barricades.

Instead, on concrete steps, lovers pose for photographs,
eyes fixed on some future moment—*It was everything
we dreamed it would be*—the purchased memory
already effacing this grey day, the hot damp air, the sweat down
warm backs, the wind-whipped smut settling in squinted eyes.

    II. Dreams (Ozu)

I dream of a wood-framed hotel in Japan, where children chatter and
mothers and daughters on final journeys prepare for sleep together,
unrolling their mats and gently folding clothes, framed perfect and scentless
in an aspect of four to three—I long for this lost and never night,
but must relinquish—like lonely mothers letting daughters go from home—
dreams in such perfect proportion.

    III. Remembering

In the last dusk blossoms cluster on trees, lie
on branches like snow fallen warm from red sky;

like drifts of snow, glow dimly in the between times light,
beauty unremembered, unrecorded in the face of this night;

reflect the final scattered photons of the day done—
as if the white blooms still hold the vanished sun.

All the men I have ever loved ride bicycles

A, with your crooked teeth and spiky hair,
Remember how we would walk beside the Liffey with your bicycle
humming and clicking as you wheeled it along
You would peel away the layers of Dublin,
Show me Viking warriors buried beneath layers of earth and stone and
    city.
When I loved you *I* re-learnt riding—pedalling with
Only a bandana on my head through the one way streets
With barely functioning brakes.
We talked about nostalgia and you said that as an archaeologist
you didn't indulge—spent
Too much time thinking about dead ice men buried in the mountains.

My belly was full of roses for you
And when I opened my mouth to speak
They twisted out like snakes
Cutting my throat and kissing your face.

B, with you I would ride slowly along the footpaths of Canberra
Or weave drunkenly down Northbourne at three am.
I smoked so many cigarettes while thinking of you that
When I opened my mouth to speak
All that came out were butts and ashes
Which you wiped from your lap with a certain tenderness.
With our bike gang we would roam the streets—
You with your long man legs and
me with my
smoker's lungs.

Once in the bus interchange I was
So drunk I fell off my bike
And we all laughed about it,
And it tasted like tears.

C, you only took up riding after we met
But with such enthusiasm that your legs ached for days.
And, with enthusiasm, you briefly loved me too.
Remember that one day we walked the streets,
And sat in coffee shops,
And I tried to show you how they kiss in old movies,
But you couldn't see why it would be any fun.
When I opened my mouth to speak
Birds flew out to delight you.

I had stopped riding then—
We never cycled together,
Or woke up together in the morning.

Then in an orchard in Turkey
On an old mountain bike with a rock hard seat
I remembered the chain whirring
And the wind in my hair.

All the men I have ever loved ride bicycles.
But in the end, a bicycle humming between your legs
Guarantees more happiness than a man.

There is a law of the universe that says
no poet dies alone

When I die I want to be attended by the ghosts of this summer evening—
what lover or friend could have a breath so cruel and gentle,
a voice so tender and unkind. I love all these claustrophobic cars passing by
blind, these houses with their windows lighted and dark that
freeze me with their warmth or seduce me with their blank eyes.
There is a poodle on the footpath and she looks at me and
tells me I will die alone and old with a terrible haircut,
attended by a blind cat and a spectre in the damp patch on the dirty wall.

Sometimes it feels like you don't want me anymore

I have a stain inside that sometimes shows.
I rake the veins that curl like vines so tight
Around my bones. I bend and bite my toes
And from my feet it flows like blood—the night
That swallows up the fire. The death wind shrieks
From empty eyes. And I have lost us all.
This road was not the one. Within your beak
I saw a curling tongue. I was enthralled.
You stripped me of my skin and naked, blind,
I sold my soul and named myself again.
I am the Hunger Ghost and I will find
You in this dark; your face will be the same.
And footless, gasping, I will come. Now moan.
And crawl with me towards the end, alone.

These days 1

These are dim days. The fires flicker out on the hills. The grass is yellow and the green has faded from the trees, but they have not yet lit their autumn flames. Are we waiting or are we dead? In the streets great silent crowds push against one another, blank eyes staring beyond the face in front of them, beyond all faces, at the glazed surface of the world. Straight, white, shining teeth purchased at the supermarket gnash at shiny baubles—none of them are gold, fool. There is no gold anymore. Wrapped in grey/white/red/the new black scratching fabrics, stitching unpicking with every step, every one of us as naked as the emperor, as blind as the emperor—all children with plastic crowns—not even rulers of our own houses, our own skin, our own muscles, our own bones. These days, there are no spaces in the air for pauses and words coagulate together on paper as people gather together in great, rotting cities. What if when Jesus died all his words clustered blood red around the holes with the nails and ran together and thickened and hardened and were lost? The imperfect memory of the apostles failed to reclaim them, and when Jesus rose his hands and feet were healed and he was no longer a man—which was the important thing. When we die they won't cover our faces with flags and call us heroes, or put us in wooden boxes and carry us through the street. Hope that they wrap you in a winding sheet and put you in the earth. One day, perhaps, this universe will be little more than a graveyard for stars.

Canberra I: An insomniac welcomes dusk, remembering harder times

There's a change coming when I
step outside—five o'clock and I've been
sleeping all through the heat of the day.
There's a breeze rising from the lake and
even though the sun's still burning I know
the evening will be cool.
Barefoot on the front step I breathe this
new day—the night coming. Sometimes it's like
I was conceived in another hemisphere and
my blood still remembers.
My skin's damp and my hair sticks to my neck—I'm
wet like a newborn baby. After
long nights drowning in memory
I saw myself reflected in a demon's eyes. I'm
real now, cut free. I'll
keep my own hours and
go walking without shoes at four am feeling
the footpath still holding yesterday's sun.

These days 2

When I was in Mexico I watched the sun setting red over the ocean and I thought whoooeee—what if it could be like this all the time? What if it could be firewheels built of sticks sparking and spitting across the sand? What if it could be dancing until dawn with your hands opened up to the sky and the moon on your face? What if it could be swimming naked in the ocean cold and salty on your skin?

When I was in your room and it was lit low and red and you were undressing for me as I lay on the bed I thought—why can't it be like this all the time? Why can't it be soft, sweet-smelling darkness? Why can't it be eyes open and mouths full of what we keep hidden from the world? Why can't it be palms pressed together and fingers and legs intertwined? Why can't it be the cool breeze on naked flesh and skin that tastes like salt after a long day in the sunshine?

When I was in the mountains I heard the silence rising off the ice and from the rocks and I thought—what if it could sound like this all the time? What if it was so quiet you could hear the stars pulsing? What if you could taste the silence and it tasted cold and fragile? What if the weight of the rocks and the weight of the earth rested on your heart and brought you peace?

When I was writing my poem and the words were gathering like crystals about a thought, around an image, and sparkling with my joy, growing like mould out of my melancholy, sharpening into a stalactite from the dripping of my tears, I thought—why can't we speak like this all the time? Why can't we speak the delicate light on the lake on a winter evening or the yearning for sunshine on your arm unmediated by energy efficient glass? Why are we fine and why is the weather nice?

When I was waiting to cross the road outside work in my suit clutching my bag with my keys and my phone and my wallet and my ID with my dimly smiling face, I watched the day slip away in an erratic stream of cars going from carport to carpark to carport again and again who knows in what direction and I thought—why is it like this most of the time?

One day the universe will collapse into nothingness—and what did you do with your apportioned days?

There are three things I have to tell you

The first is that this world is a world of nails and ice cream
barbed wire hung with flags of skin and trillions of trees breathing
beautiful strangers with great hair and soldiers
with their hands in the dust and blood on their shoes
a world where new skyscrapers and
fresh ruins are made every day

In your hand this morning as you woke from sleep you held
four cat videos and the photo of a boy dead on a beach
and outside it was spring and
the wattles were blooming

You wanted to write a poem about this but you
would sound like a wanker
because poems try to make these things fit together
and the first thing I have to tell you is
the world is broken and you can't make it whole

The second thing I have to tell you is that the stars are really far away
and when you look at them you look into the past

And I have a lover and if he dies before me I will
put my body into suspended animation
until time travel is invented and then I will wake again
and travel back to before we met
and meet him first
and we will be lovers for the first time again
and this has already happened
so when he looks at me sometimes
he remembers who I will be

And the second thing I have to tell you is the stars are really far away
and when they flicker they
telegraph the passing moments
in the most comforting way
make time seem less fixed
our loves and grief less finite

The third thing I have to tell you is that most of your poems
end at the ocean
even when you live far from the sea
and you will try to write new poems but you just say the same thing
over and over again but slightly differently
and that in itself is kind of like the ocean on a shore
with the waves hushing or hissing or crashing again and again different
and the same
so now the ocean is sort of wrapped up in this poem

But the ocean itself is not a poem
a poem is when you were a child crouched with your feet in the
warm shallows
touching the foam with your fingertips
a poem is when the wave picked you up and
tossed you
and held you under the water so long
you knew that if you inhaled you would fill with water and
become the continuous water

Even now you are walking in a land bound city as darkness is falling
and you see a broken branch lying across the path
and you pick it up and hold it in your hand
and it is the hand that held the picture of the dead boy
and the tree is still whole but this is no comfort to the fallen branch
and the stars are starting to come out
and your lover is waiting for you at home
and the ending of that is far ahead and far behind

and your poem is broken
but even this far inland time is a continuous whole
just makes a different sound
as each moment
breaks on you

And the third thing I have to tell you is that all poems begin and
end with the ocean
because they are the sound of the living earth which exceeds us
and limits us
is our beginning and our end
always breaking always whole
is what I tell myself

2.
April makes fools of us all

The inside of her

She spends her nights beside the red lamp, making
finger puppet figures on her bedroom wall.

She sleeps alone, with three pillows and
paper spread like rubble across her sheets.

She walks to the bus stop barefoot, but
puts on her shoes before anyone sees.

These things are all that was left to her—
and two days in autumn when

the sun falls at a certain angle on
the inside of her skin.

Babushka

I fold the world into me—those cyclists
in the distance riding slowly through the eucalypts,
I pick up the earth underneath them and
fold them into me—their going slowly, going
nowhere in particular, breathing the air,
I fold into me, and they cycle on along
the hills and valleys of my ribcage,
feeling the slow wind of my breath moving the earth—
you standing across the room, I
pick up the faded carpet under your feet and
fold you into me—you nestle in my belly
where it is warm, and hear my heart thudding
above your head—your love and grief and anger
mixes with my blood—I fold the world
into me—those concrete buildings smudging the sky
—I pick up the dirty road beside them and
fold them into me, where they cram against
my liver, my kidneys, my spine,
cutting my guts—my blood and bone
wears them down—they crumble—and I
piss them out onto the earth—those
shuttered houses full of shuttered people—
I pick up the emptiness that surrounds them
and fold them into me, where the acids of my body
dissolve their walls, and all the people swim out—
riding the waves of my blood from my heart
to my fingers to my heart to my toes
to my heart to my scalp
—swimming together naked, laughing—I fold the world
into me, and it devours me—me in the world

the world in me.

Elegy

The mirror gives back only my
inverted self. The night is cold,
like hands or kisses. Perhaps
stars feel like flowers
in some infinite universe,
not this one.

Startup program WMN-12000

I will be any kind of woman for you
A buttercup woman
A goatherd woman
A woken at three am smiling woman
An in your bed woman
A hairy-legged femo-lesbian woman
An open wound woman
A Brazilian-waxed fake-tan woman
A glacial woman
A rock cut through by retreating ice, scarred and ancient woman
A having breakfast standing up naked in your kitchen woman
A crying on the bus woman
A donkeys in the field ran too far and too fast woman
An aeroplane trail across the sky woman
A laughing in the movies when no one else does woman
A lentils and rice woman
An abandoned bag at the station woman
A duty free woman
A gluten free woman
A stranger singing somewhere on a moonless night woman
A paperclip woman
A saucepan woman
A let the mouse down gently on a ribbon woman
A stones in your back when you're sleeping woman
A keeping the dream alive woman
A who are you anyway woman
A lapis lazuli woman
A pearl necklace breaking in the water woman
A darkness falling woman
A purple woman
A far far away but still faithful woman
I will be any kind of woman for you
Just enter the program number listed in your manual and press OK

some days in autumn my poems don't tell stories

rains all week life lurches on
drunken heavy mornings dark
days fill with screens bright
sharp lines jar soft grey sky
water blurring windowpanes

drops gather surfaces objects
boundaries substance porous
life lurches confused circles
bed midday warm suspended
dark curtain treacles time

life sings mutters a tale goes
nowhere refuses stories resists
plot narrative meaning favours
puddle growing shrinking
tree heavy with inedible apples

supermarket bright magazines
clash with day never brightens
comes goes imperceptibly denies
beginning end impossible white
smiles glossy skin so clear it hurts

distance between us the world
clear some weeks in autumn
clouds roll in we turn in to see
tears gather on inside of skin
shadows gather round bones

life stumbles drunk cannot stand
bright lights loud voices inside
outside night lies on ground
breathing sleeping all that are left
can't make a story anymore

Inside the city it has no name

in the morning the traffic noises start and
it rains a lot of the time i go searching for
coffee and breakfast on the train we
sway in unison and standing by the canal

i think there is this and there is the Story i will tell

Canberra III: all tonight's parties

tonight we have an extra hour—for riding to parties, perhaps—smell of sausages and the sound of voices from a balcony above—the celebration of a mirage of extra time—in that apartment block I went to a party and someone threw up in a flowerpot and someone else emptied the dirt and vomit down onto the pavement below—it turned out to be a worm farm—now the smell of sausages and the sound of voices—something warming—in the air, in the sounds of strangers—from the balcony of my party I can look up and see figures standing by a window and the flash of cameras—the night is full—on limestone avenue a whole house glows and sings and don't its darkened neighbours seem content to let it shout—knowing we can sleep for an extra hour—I am passing by the people walking into the city for dancing and drinking before the cold comes and the dark days shut us away—this warmth the gift of March before April makes fools of us all—time slows around you—and this is one of those nights when everyone's party lets you in

Copan, the ruins

Once, I wrote letters, but found
the silent replies too much to bear.
Declarations and explanations are unimportant,
it seems. I saw myself in a mirror
for the first time in a month.
Perhaps I had changed a little.
I put my hand on my stomach
and thought that my nakedness
was for myself only;
it did not have to be unbeautiful.
I have stood like this before a great many people,
worn out and factory-made. In the mirror,
in all the eyes that looked on me.
No more letters. Words cannot
draw out a reflection from a face.
Poems are made for silence.
The acts are done, the words are said, the
things inside are broken. Before the mirror
I gathered up those plain and heavy limbs.
Once, I stripped myself onto paper.
These days, I wear shadows and tears.

The Opposing Shore (after Julien Gracq)

The mist rises from the wetlands and wreathes the goalposts—
thickened air blurs the stars—(they won't see you []) familiar is
around, behind, but not ahead. See how the mist draws a
line in the air and beyond the line is another place, an
opposing shore that whispers strangely in a voice like []
tears gathered behind your eyes, the ache of your tongue for
[] how I pursue through the night, down the
winding path; this foreign place where [] how I long to
feel with my hand outstretched before me the air change and
thicken, become substantial underneath my fingers—I ache
with longing to [] transgress that invisible line
which is always one step ahead; like

drunks spilling out into the night finding the air
thick with meaning like molasses; sticking to faces, to throats;
lips tremble to be kissed so [] forcefully by the world. Stepping
out they raise their hands to grab this voluptuous night and [] oh
she eludes them somehow; the air is heavy with *alludes to* her but their
trembling arms are still empty. *Let's roll on* let's roll on after her
one more (time) one more glass will surely rent the veil entirely and
the dark fairy queen will come and take us as [] *Bite me, scratch me,
rend me* (who whispers? me/you/her) let the night transgress our flesh and
take us like [] take us as her *slaves/lovers/food* till we are
no longer separated from one another like

flesh and world and others are now. Blood longs for air calls so
urgently from tingling veins and [] (rend your flesh) transgress this
paper (skin) thin wall between the world and [] all that is
inside will come out and you will be nothing anymore *please I want* []
flesh longs for touch—I am porous, reaching; if our skin touches
the charge will dissolve me and I will [] Always still one step ahead
the boundary of you the permeable/impermeable quantum state
of your longing for me. The mist encircles and everywhere is
other and I spin with my fingers out but
the line cannot be [] the night will not be [] and I cannot []

transgress/ed.

Boxes

It is night and it is raining and the streetlights are shining off the road
    so I
can't see the lanes, only a wide black path glowing white
at regular intervals. What if this asphalt highway marked with suns
took us up into the sky, above ourselves? Twisting through the clouds,
heavy with water, my senses would be muffled and I could
take a moment to look away and look at you; take my hands off the
    wheel
and touch your leg. In the close, damp clouds perhaps the fog would
    fill me
and there would be less empty space in which to lose myself in hollow
    screaming.
In the quiet, dense air, perhaps you would be quieter and cooler and
floating above the world less heavy with the world, with remembering
    and forgetting.
In the clouds our palms would be damp when they touched,
and our breath would make tiny new clouds in the air.
If this road was surfaced with night and suns we would be supermen,
burning with love and freezing with grief, swimming through space in
    silent exaltation.
Not in a box with wheels in the rain, sitting in silence, our love and
    our grief in boxes.

Your rock at the end of the world

There is a rock at the end of the world, one
for each of us, for us to
gather together what is left.
On your rock,
there will be nothing left of me.
You will be frowning, and your shirt
will smell of washing powder.

Yesterday, I pressed my face into your chest
put my hand on your stomach.
Yesterday, we fucked in the darkness.

Loving sits on the palm of the world in a strong wind,
is as nothing
in the face of grief or anger or
living.

I will not be with you on your rock at the end of the world.
I am not with you today.

The world on Sir J Herschel's Projection
by John Bartholomew

In this fairy tale, it is morning and we wake and
the sky is
    cracking open and our embrace is insufficient,
it seems, to hold things together anymore, to
keep the stars alight.
                Outside, the frost lies
so thick on dirt, on grass, on leaves, on houses
still slumbering and cars left to their dreams;
renders drivers blind and drives
caterpillars into blind cocoons.
                But the frost is not thick
or cold enough to freeze time, to keep the earth from breaking.

In this fairy tale, the wallpaper is white with yellow roses,
and reminds us of the olden days when things were real and whole—
we woke with the sun and killed our own pigs and
made our own cheese from the milk from our own cows
and knitted scarves by the fire in the evening made from
wool from our own sheep.
              The wallpaper is white with
yellow roses, like in the olden days, but the paper
shifts and bulges, un-real, haunted by the dark thing
that whispers and waits, sharpening its teeth,
waiting for the cracks to appear.

In this fairy tale, knowing what the Earth looks like from space
has not prevented the stars from going out one by one
as we turned the lights on at home.
                This fairy tale is in fast forward
as buildings rise and fall like ages have passed, not time but us
shaping the world and wearing it down, in this fairy tale we
wake and sleep and wake and sleep and fast forward is like

pause:
        under the frost this world is a placid lake
concealing fearsome monsters which rage and churn,
nightmares made flesh and bone and teeth.
The World on Sir J Herschel's Projection fails to capture
the new shape of this Earth. Our fairy tales,
our stories, are
        breaking at the
edges, from the inside, however artfully
we design our lines and images and
meter and rhyme. This fairy tale is
        broken, is
haunted
  by monsters that will not be
vanquished.
              Stirring under the wallpaper,
white with yellow roses, not like the
olden days, when things were real, were whole—

now teeth and whispers that
our warmth, our dreams cannot
    keep at bay.

3.
The smell of salt

Drinks and chats with old friends

Of the past I would say that I had to learn kissing again—
I'd been trying to do it hiding the wounds on my lips.
Nobody ever told me that was a problem.
These days, all of this small life of mine
floods into a moment, the pupil of my eye
quivers and bursts and bleeds black through my skin
(makes me look a little strange in well-lit rooms).
On the Staten Island Ferry one evening I saw
Manhattan vanish and then reappear. It made the whole
being thing seem a little less serious.
This skin is the same because it remembers
unformed touches. Did I ever tell you?
I have a worm inside me
that eats despair and shits out love.

The first frost of winter we did not sleep well

The frost is growing outside
        in crystals along the
                hills-hoist wires, growing
inside, flowering along
        branching nerves and
                fracturing sleep and time

The frost is growing outside
    in perfect incisors
        on the windowsill
            and inside
                the jagged night
                    clamps my mind
so still that time changes state, solidifies

No longer an
    unfathomed liquid river
        carrying me down
time halts
    and holds me tight
        in a million simultaneous frozen fingers
holds me

There, I am
      staring through a plane window
      trembling on the edge of arriving
        knowing
        knowing this moment is
            ending
            not ended
            will pass

                be remembered

                              passed
And here you are
                there you were
                      not even a ghost
                              but a stranger
time changes state
   and behind are moments
       set in ice like glass

Outside the frost suspends
                    in perfect crystals
and time has changed state

   Ahead the ice is black
     with tight-wove nets
        of frozen threads
             that might not be

I know all
     nothing
        know only that this
will be passed
              pass
                    only the river
ends in an unmapped ocean
                only I carry this crystal
      when the river flows

It will quiver against these others I found
   hum as I hear your feet climb the stairs
      wrapped in your own icy haunting I would
         wrap you instead in

this that I found in the frost—

The road up the coast wound past small houses
    and sea-salted trees
        from the bus we saw
            grey waves
                smash on cliffs turning
                    broken faces to the
                        afternoon sun
amazing you

And you held my hand smiling even though you were afraid

Atlantis

Cities sigh past us like rain
these days and
we hear only condemnation
from the lips of foreign rivers.
God has not forgiven, for
even friends forget
in the face of their own desire.

Washington does not inquire
after Athens, Vienna, Babylon.
On the banks of the Potomac
we too think that we remember,
like in Paris in the Spring,
the Seine lent us beauty,
or so we believed.

And when the sky fell,
shedding flakes of white skin,
we dreamt our souls were purified.
The earth curves.
The land will show us home.

But the plane never lands
and the angels fly by us,
seeking heaven.

The Lady Vanishing

Late nights: in
black and white (The Lady
Vanishes—I've
seen this one before). I always
missed the big nights, but
I've seen a lot of
old films. No one
kisses like that
any more, no one
knows how, and men
never grow pencil moustaches.
Even if I
dreamed myself sexy
like a movie star, and
drank coloured cocktails
through pink-sticked lips,
the night wouldn't
split open like
the stars hinted and
I heard once in a dream.
There is no
inside to this out—
just Michael Redgrave's moustache
and the English taking tea. Imagine
kissing without tongues in
a 1950s cab—the
dry lips of the night
make a promise that after
(fade to black)
it will be
undreamt, unspeakable.

.

Travelling is nothing like a poem

Grey is nothing like longing.
Brief sunshine nothing like a dream of home.
The rain drove through my jumper on an
empty train platform.
I can count days but not raindrops.
Nights are more not less lonely.
He is never sleeping when I am.

Ghosts and ashes

The surface of the night is the surface of an eye.
Winter waits in the cold September night.
I am walking alone, sleeping alone.
Summer is coming where my love is—
he will be waking now.

Longing stretches me across the oceans—
thin as a fingernail I vanish into the dark of the city.
I am afraid I have stirred memories.
I am afraid of the distance to his arms,
measured in seconds, measured in metres.

The train is light inside,
the darkness outside is a hundred other darknesses.
Zombie corpses of my old griefs
tear the scars that marked their graves on my skin.
They hear my feet retracing old roads.

Who knows what I will see in the city—
it is not a tomb, and does not know me.
My lover's arms are flesh and bones.
I will go home and in silence he will take me
back into the earth again.

Hold me tight.

The late night thoughts of a small-minded woman

On the TV they're speaking Spanish in an old American movie
and I'm eating corn chips and guacamole. It reminds me of
a bus station in San Antonio where I dreamed that
I would be shiny like a star, or a sequined dress. I would be
beautiful and thin and loved more.

But I got too hungry.

What story to tell? At the moment I'm liking
party girl with dark pupils that turn inside out when she
looks at the moonless sky. She wears lipstick sometimes, but it
smudges off on beer glasses, and runs into the dry gullies around
    her mouth.
I want to drink too much and smoke too many cigarettes and
vomit on the street, wipe my mouth and smile.

All crying like babies inside.

If my waist was smaller, perhaps my life would not be
so different, but at least I wouldn't have to
sleep with ugly men. And with
the handsome ones I wouldn't always be
reaching to turn out the lights.
(In the dark they all look the same.)

I would still give love in great bloody rivers.

I will continue to fail in all my goals; I only wish my failures were great
enough to make them art. Perhaps I could be a Texas country song—

I bite and I'm bitten,
I drink and I'm dead.
And I've got blood on my teeth
after giving you head.

If I was a moon I would be waning not waxing—
weeping and voluptuous and looking on darkness.

Second person

You were the kind of person whose
name people forgot—even your
face was the same as a number of
other faces, to the extent that it was
unmemorable and could be passed by
by the passer-by in the street.

As a child, no one ever
came to your birthday parties,
and finally you stopped having them.
For a time you felt an affinity
with uranium, until you discovered
that half-life was a measure of
time, not quality.

You travelled, took photos, even took
lovers, who forgot your name and the
feel of your skin and the touch of your hand
so quickly. You would know yourself
virginal even lying in a sticky post-coital
embrace, still unknown. Nobody ever
regretted your absence in a
melancholy moment, years to come.

You lived with others and then
alone. In effect it was much the same;
the world ignoring you was just
situated at a different distance from
the body that even you doubted.
At work, people seemed to think that
the things you did just happened.
Your presence or absence went
largely unremarked.

You wrote poems which dissipated
even as you spoke them.
The stage lights left you in shadow.
The microphone amplified nothing.
You painted pictures of the clouds
coming down to kiss the ocean and
then burnt them in homage to
intransience and the unknown.

Your life was long, and full of
events which largely passed you by.
But you watched them passing and
noted every detail. You remembered
every lover and loved each one.
You notched no bedposts,
made no records for posterity.

When you were old, each day
you celebrated with a smile
thousands of unmarked anniversaries,
took small walks and looked around.
This is your epitaph—you remembered
up until the moment you forgot.

Epilogue

Strange days in new places I find myself thinking—weren't there
other things I used to say? I hold my silence in the palm of my hand, in
a room which holds none of the trappings that in old times I
used to draw around me. My tongue
quivers sometimes on the edge of speaking, like lips
on the edge of kissing after a long time alone.

I tremble, but we see only the movement of the leaves and not the wind;
only a few take the time to sit and, making their ears a shell, listen to the
keening of the solitary air. Through time does the beauty retreat
to the cage of dark lines on printed pages, leaving the mouth hungry
after the meal is eaten and the cigarettes are smoked? It is not
such a wonder that some lovers bite to draw blood.

When longing remembers for us, our minds collect dreams: my
face resting on a warm shoulder and all the speaking has been
done, there are so few now who wander the streets searching for
the places where the world comes undone. I seek
the comfort of eyes that too have seen those cracks. Perhaps
we have hidden too well, wearing silence and carrying always

the beginning of a cry whose words we do not know.

Like a fish on a wire

At the end of the Earth there is a cliff and
some people are born facing the haunted ocean—
grey waves rent through with darkness and
crested with fallen stars. You will know them by
the smell of salt on their skin and the scars on
the inside of their eyes. If I see you there I will
hold you however you want me to—tie you down.
But I will never ask you to be happy, or to
remain a human being for me, if you would rather
be a fish and leap off the edge of this world.

4.
Seekers of the emergency exit

Mexico D.F.

Sitting in a café in Mexico City where Che Guevara and Fidel Castro
    plotted revolution
I fail to plot anything
No longer believing in world domination
Preferring perhaps to be dominated
Weighed down by the stones of a strange city I find pleasure in the sharp
    stings of loneliness

No one sees more clearly, no one sees at all clearly

Crushed into a train with somebody's crotch rubbing against my leg I know
This is all the touching we ever get and I am
So tired of strangers and the touch of their skin in buses and
The cry of their voices in the streets
We are all strangers with our eyes fixed on our own souls
We can never meet in the streets or in our guarded houses

I sit alone in a small hotel room with its one bed and a sink for my hand
    and
I believe myself to be abandoned
Fear that I have run too far

And I look out onto alien rooftops at sunset through my broken window
Dream of homecomings that exist only in my mind
Know them to be dreams
I will feel pleasure at the pain of leaving
And the memory of what was lost
And what was withheld
I love the bruising hand of the indifferent world on my soul
Those that have come to hate me
Those that never knew me
Those that beat my heart with distance and with absence
And with the failure of their love

And in a café in Mexico City I too plan a revolution

In which I no longer cry, except in sad movies,
Or bleed, except onto paper in secret rooms at four am
Stop watching any TV that makes me believe
That happiness exists and is necessary and is the absence of pain
And I will stop spreading my soul at the feet of strangers because

Silence is the gift we give to our sorrow

The Idiot (Savannah nights)

In March on a cold spring night I came into Savannah
watching glowing headlights from the window of the bus—
I came to paint the town
I bought a new belt with a shiny buckle and six cans of bad beer, just because they
leapt out at me from the fridge at 7-Eleven
I drank one as I walked

In the bus station bathroom I made myself
beautiful with only green eyeliner and pink lipstick
and pulled out some cleavage from my
light-weight low-cut black top
I put my bag in a locker and
sashayed out into the southern night—
stars are fairy lights and
the road shines with remembered rain

In a bar a man asked me what I did with myself
                and I told him
I was taking Unhappiness out for the night
He asked me why?

                and I said that
I liked to show Unhappiness a good time because then he
whispered me secrets as we walked home and
in the dark he undressed me, un-
buckled me and because I was
beautiful he
flayed my skin and
stretched my bones until I
forgot them all

and cried out tearless and demon-eyed

sort of a map of me

I am sort of the colour of angels, or
the inside of lips stained with red wine.
My mind moves as slowly as a tortoise:
as old and as in tune with the movement of the tides.
In the distance, I hear laughing and
people playing fiddles to the moon.
While some nights I have loved dancing—
my body moving like a marionette whose
happiness comes from powerlessness—I find myself
never coming to your parties
or answering your calls. Despite claims to the contrary
some of us were born with better maps to this time.
Remember those who are lost are wandering roads
long past, or tracks in the sky yet to be built.

In the carpark of tomorrow we can all find a parking space

In the carpark of tomorrow, you will never have trouble finding a space.
The cars produce no fumes, and we can all breathe freely,
even with the windows down: put your head out the window and see.
(At higher altitudes, breathing apparatus may be required,
but the views of the carpark are excellent.)

The lower basement levels are well heated by the
proximate core of the Earth. (But keep your eyes out for the
Old Ones woken from their slumber.) Take your towels when
visiting the tropics—turn off the air conditioning for a
private sauna in your vehicle. At the Poles, the carpark sometimes
freezes—but use your heater with caution, lest you
defrost an alien from a distant star.

Levels are coded by number, colour, continent and letters from
various alphabets. Everyone is issued a ticket at birth.
It is rumoured that if sufficient change is inserted into the machine,
your ticket will be validated, and will open one of the exit doors.

Exits are rumoured to lead to a beautiful garden—
moist and verdant and humming with invisible life—
or to a desert marred with the stone of ruined cities
or to The Shopping Centre or The Mall.
Most believe they lead to the mystical Valet Parking Section.

The Seekers of the Emergency Exit who wander the stairs of the fire
    escapes,
always up or always down, speak simply of The Street.
And a few longing souls, stealing their first kiss against a concrete pillar
or pressed into a doorway of a broken lift, might whisper of the ocean—
the carpark must halt in the face of the sea, my love; we will stand
with the waves around our ankles and stare at the stars.

(But from the cracks in the concrete, the carpark weeps salty tears,
and the walls seem sometimes to contain
the outline of a whale, a starfish, the spiralling lines of anenomes.)

Glory be to you who sung
(with Gerard Manley Hopkins)

Glory be to you, who sung the beauty of
all things counter, original, spare, strange—
you thanking God, I thank you, hearing your
springing rhythm singing *this morning*
morning's minion as I see the eagle up
above the mountain riding *rung upon*
the rein of a wimpling wing against the
sunset sky—smooth pink marked with
uneven orange ridges; I hear your delight in
pied beauty, *skies of couple colour*. But more,
hear your *heart in hiding*, hear the distance from the *king-*
dom of daylight's dauphin to your
heart stirring in darkness. How I first heard
you speak of the mountains of the mind, *frightful,*
sheer, no man fathomed, and wonder
even now at how your poems soar like the
dapple-dawn-drawn Falcon while mine flap and
caw like clumsy cockatoos, or hop along like
heavy ravens picking at the earth. And how
when my cries *on an age old anvil wince and sing* my
heart hops heavy towards you—to the comfort
you offer (*serves in a whirlwind*) that
each day dies with sleep. O, did you find
freedom from your *bone house, mean house*, cage
of flesh? O, know then that when I *wake and feel the*
fell of dark not day, I hold your singing close and know
other hearts have hidden in these mountains,
wept to be human in this cage, not meadow-down a
rainbow stands upon. Where you lie, I
know you think not of your bones nor
sadness; having found your relief. *All life death*
does end; and as this day ends, I think of you.

The journey out

You are on a train, going west, and the west is waiting for you, violent and expectant and full of gold, and you have a hat and a gun and a troubled past, shadows making strange shapes in dirty rooms and the clink of cheap glasses, a daughter left behind with an old woman in a house with no light or running water left with only a promise of return you fear you will never keep, and you have made yourself again from lace and broken bed springs and scraped a new face from the ice on the east coast roads, and your garter is stuffed with firecrackers and grief and the fingers of dead men.

You are on a boat, heading south, and the south is waiting for you, violent and expectant and full of gold, and you have a troubled past obscured by London fog with hints of knives bared and bodies sinking beneath the treacle water of the Thames, and you have made yourself again from seaweed and broken bottles emptied of messages, and scraped a face from dead fish and whale songs, and your stockings are stuffed with the bread you stole and a stone you found among the rubbish on the muddy bank of the river.

You are on a bicycle, heading north and the north is not waiting for you, is indolent and empty and full and you have made yourself again from the sand between your toes and the steam from afternoon rain on hot roads, and you have scraped a face from a hint you took from the mirror this morning, and your shorts are stuffed with autumn leaves and burning pyres of car tyres and cracking ice cliffs plunging into the ocean at the edge of the end of the world.

You are on a spaceship heading out, and the galaxy is waiting for you, violent and empty and full of dark energy, and you have no past on a scale that matters to the stars, and you have made yourself again from photons and electricity, and scraped a face from space junk and old radio transmissions, and your space suit is stuffed with a small portion of missing dark matter of which you remain unaware and the last flower that bloomed on Earth you pressed between the pages of an empty book.

she walks the long way home

she walks the long way home—the only time she finds for writing (invisible) verses on the skin of the world—tracing (burning) lines across the flesh of (disintegrating) lovers carving a (terrible) pattern across the face of the world with her wandering—now she is (ruined) gathering fragments—listening to her breath moving confirming that the blood moves in her body, this mass of flesh and water built from stars and darkness is still (unified) here—she searches her mind for the day gone but finds only a (dim) outline of a stranger sitting, staring as the world grows darker—memories she shores against impending annihilation by a series of (anaesthetic) tomorrows

(fade to black)

remembers sleeping in a bus, her cheek against the window (knowing) a mass of bones and muscle and veins wrapped delicately in this fine pale skin—journeys through March days still chilly, in a bus station (waiting) in Texas, in Louisiana, in Georgia, she is alone, a seven-dimensional universe packaged tightly in a down jacket (yearning) seeking unification with space and time—in Savannah she drank blue-ribbon beer from a can and planned (desiring) to scale the wall of a cemetery where the dead lie marked and forgotten—

(fade to black)

in New Orleans she conquered time and saw (painted on the toilet wall) the desert burning and monstrous cities growing and the children of tomorrow (after the apocalypse) do not forgive or blame but forget, wielding the eternal present and loving and killing and dying (we cannot imagine)—she breakfasted on eggs and grits watching the river flow—before the levees broke (she could not imagine) after she had gone

(fade to black)

now she walks the long way home from work (active) where
destruction comes slowly—eyes bleeding into computer screens in
an office with tinted windows (employed), the world grows dim, and
memories are wares lined up in a shop window to show the world
(well-travelled) and she grows tired and sees no more visions
the universe inside her collapsed and reborn in a lizard's eye

(fade to black)

once she was a poet—now she walks the long way home, breathing
smoke, trying to lose herself and find the path again that took her out
of time, where the darkness is painted red with fire and the people
stride through eleven dimensions, loving and killing and dying—she
tries to leave herself behind in darkening streets, steps quickening,
the pale shadow she has become slowing, fading, falling, while she
that *knew* and *saw* and *moved*, knows and sees and moves—mounting
the wave of time she plunges into the infinite, eternal, simultaneous
ocean—and before she reaches her front door she has danced with
Alberich to the tune of the Nibelungs' hammers and built a spaceship
from their gold, flown across the galaxy and mined the empty rivers
of Mars to build great cities just to grind them down again, swum the
Acheron to dine with Hades in the Spring, and picnicked in the ruins
of Valhalla on a fine day in April, among giant butterflies, watching
the sun die

(fade to black)

she walks the long way home, to slip the chains of space and time,
of *was* and *is* and *must always be*—she is running now, casting off her
things—she was a poet once, a lover, a worker, a traveller, a dancer—
now—

(the Fool takes the stage)

—*Poets! Throw down your pens!* Take up your knives!—The only poems
that survive us are the ones we carve on the skin of the world!

(lights up)

A song, the world to come

I. Wandering

If you were to paint this spring you would paint it blue and green—
intense and sun-filled, the warm afternoon like honey on my tongue
    and in my belly.
There was a poet once who sang the body electric, and I too want to
    sing—
my body, the new leaves and their tender veins, the heavy roses,
the warm movement of the air—
sing this day electric and eternal.

I am walking—my legs move, the joints click and swing, blood
coursing through arteries, capillaries bringing the sweet spring air
to my flexing muscles, my tingling skin.
Wandering across the soft grass my genius is to
remove my shoes and to feel the prickles of the blades and the softness
    of the earth.

When you lay down to die it is days like this you will linger on
when you wandered and built nothing, made nothing, destroyed
    nothing—
entirely present in the heavy-lidded joy of breathing, of walking,
of tasting the air and hearing the
molecules shifting as the world grew and dissolved.

And I would wander too, not just across the skin of the world,
but across my lover's skin,
tracing my route from the soft folds around his eyes
down across his beard which prickles like the grass
to the bone of his hip which I kiss in wonder
at how we fit together.

And I whisper to him that in the future, the roots will crack the roads
and bicycle bells will say only hello and good day and never get out of
    the way
and we breathe from each other's lips and surely it will only be
    tomorrow.

II. Flying

The birds that rest on the wind above the grey, wrinkled ocean
feel the shifting of their feathers, the pulse of their heart,
the vertical movement of their wings.
The birds' eyes see the ocean, and the mountains rising up capped with snow
against the clouded sky, and the bird never says bird, mountain, ocean, rock, home.
But we standing, can fill ourselves with the angle of the peak,
the black and the white, the
terror of the sharpness, the heaviness of the rock, the movement of the Earth
by a millimetre a year,
the salty depths, the pale sun and the Earth wheeling in the expanses of the universe.
We, wandering, can fill ourselves with the world—with the
fluttering heart of the warm bird flying.

III. Dying

But we, building, earning, making our name are filled with nothing, will die hollow—
the price of our name on a stone, in a book.
And I tell you that in the future, the men who would reject a lover because her breasts sagged or her forehead creased or her cunt was too hairy or its lips too long,
and the women who would reject a lover because his
belly was too big or his hair was too thin or his bank balance too small,
will die old and grinning, destroyed by their robot lovers
who mutilated their own perfect plastic skins
in an endeavour to become more human.

III. Singing

I sing the wanderings, the unnamed, sad eyelids, the ingenuity of joints—
and while my song will not be remembered, I will continue
in the grass, in the shivering air, in eternal impermanence,
as the earth, the sea, the bird, the stars.

Afterword

George Eliot wrote that a poet's soul is one 'in which knowledge passes instantaneously into feeling, and feeling flashes back as a new organ of knowledge'. I don't believe in the soul, but this idea of poetry as being a translator between knowledge and feeling appeals to me. The works of literature I love the most gesture beyond themselves and back at the world. Art should attempt to make us look up from the object and to look at the world differently. I try to write a poem that bursts with living, like Walt Whitman, or springs with strange rhythms, like Gerard Manley Hopkins, or dissects everyday life with disparate symbols, like Sylvia Plath. But when I write a poem, the poem almost always fails to capture the knowledge, express the feeling. It might be a moment in time, a scene, an idea. But the shape of the words is never quite right. In the translation between knowledge and feeling and back something of both it lost. I think the words should express that too. I want my poems to lack, fail, make space for what is missing.

About the Author

Miranda Lello lives in Canberra where she has been writing and performing poetry for the past fifteen years. This is her first poetry collection. She writes about poetry and other things on her blog mirandalello.wordpress.com where early versions of some of these poems first appeared.

Acknowledgements

I would like to thank Shane Strange from Recent Work Press for publishing this book, and all the work he and Alice Beecham put into reading, re-reading, editing and laying out. It is a much better book for all the thoughtful comments you both provided. Thanks to all the people around Canberra who have supported my poetry for so many years: Julian, whose poetry slam kept me writing even after I started full time work, including many of the poems in this book; Andrew, who over the years has offered me the chance to feature at lots of Canberra poetry events; Aaron, Fiona, Zoe and Brown Owl for giving feedback from the sucking void; and everyone who has invited me to perform or found something in my poems to like. Apologies to Alex for creating such a large poetry debt and bringing you small misfortunes. And finally to my muses: Anthony, who for almost twelve years has been part of my poetry; Canberra, in the good times and the bad; and bicycles.

"To Mr Charles Bukowski" was first published in *Block #2* (2006); "Copan: the ruins" was shortlisted for the *2007 ACT Poetry Prize;* "The late night thoughts of a small minded woman" was first published in *Burley* (2012); "Boxes" was first published in *fourW twenty three;* "Babushka" and "A Song, the World to Come" were first published in *Dazzled: University of Canberra Vice-Chancellor's International Poetry Prize 2014;* "The Opposing Shore" was first published in *Axon: Creative Explorations* No. 5 (2015)

'Glory be to you who sung' uses lines from "The Windhover", "Pied Beauty", "No Worst, There is None", "The Caged Skylark" by Gerard Manly Hopkins.

2016 Editions

Pulse Prose Poetry Project
Incantations Subhash Jaireth
Transit Niloofar Fanaiyan
Gallery of Antique Art Paul Hetherington
Sentences from the Archive Jen Webb
River's Edge Owen Bullock

2017 Editions

A Song, the World to Come Miranda Lello
Members Only Melinda Smith and Caren Florance
The future, un-imagine Angela Gardner and Caren Florance
The Bulmer Murder Paul Munden
Cities: Ten Poets, Ten Cities Various
Dew and Broken Glass Penny Drysdale
Proof Maggie Shapley
Soap Charlotte Guest
Isolator Monica Carroll
Icarus Paul Hetherington
Work & Play Owen Bullock

all titles available from
www.recentworkpress.com

www.ingramcontent.com/pod-product-compliance
Lightning Source LLC
Chambersburg PA
CBHW020624300426
44113CB00007B/768